Too Many Frogs!

By Michele Spirn
Illustrated by Ye Wan

Scott Foresman
is an imprint of

Glenview, Illinois • Boston, Massachusetts • Chandler, Arizona •
Upper Saddle River, New Jersey

Photographs

Every effort has been made to secure permission and provide appropriate credit for photographic material. The publisher deeply regrets any omission and pledges to correct errors called to its attention in subsequent editions.

Unless otherwise acknowledged, all photographs are the property of Pearson Education, Inc.

12 Frank Greenaway/©DK Images.

ISBN 13: 978-0-328-50856-3
ISBN 10:   0-328-50856-X

5 6 7 8 9 10 V010 13 12

Josh looked around his room. It looked good. It was painted his favorite color—blue. He loved everything in his room. He had many toys, books, and games. But something was missing. It was too quiet and lonely.

"It's too lonely here. I really want a pet," Josh said to his mother. "Then my room wouldn't be lonely."

"You can save your money and buy a pet," said Mom. "Or maybe we can find a pet. We can go down to the pond tomorrow."

Josh went to bed thinking about a pet. That night he dreamed he was hiking in a beautiful coral-colored canyon. He heard the whisper of the wind in the bushes. The wind made the bushes sway and blew slivers of rock all around. He heard the rattle of a rattlesnake and saw a lizard shoot across the sand. Josh woke up and thought about the animals in his dream. *I'll never find the right pet*, he thought.

That morning, Josh told Mom about his
dream as they walked to the town pond
to have a picnic. Josh helped Mom set up
their lunch. Then, all of a sudden, they saw
something hop. It was a frog. Josh ran after
it and caught it. "This is a great pet, Mom,"
Josh said. They took it home. Josh called the
frog Hoppy.

Hoppy was so much fun that Josh asked
Mom if they could go back to the pond.
Josh found more frogs. He brought home
Hoppy 2 and Hoppy 3. The day after that he
brought home Hoppy 4, Hoppy 5, Hoppy 6,
Hoppy 7, and Hoppy 8.

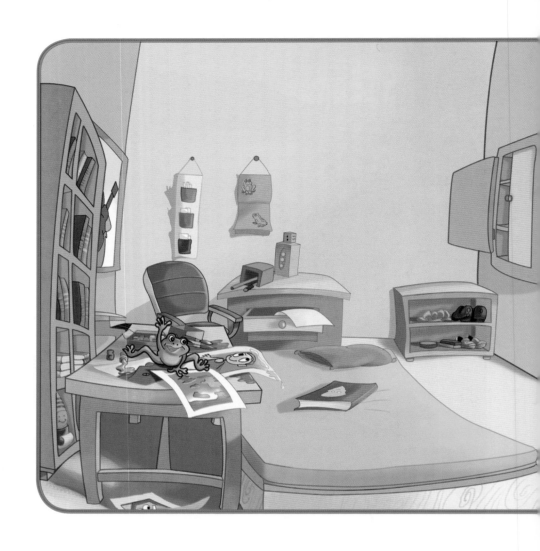

Then one day Hoppy 6 jumped on Mom's head when she walked into Josh's room. "Eeek," she cried. "There are too many pets in this house!"

What did Mom mean? thought Josh. He had changed his room from being lonely to being filled with pets. Wasn't that good?

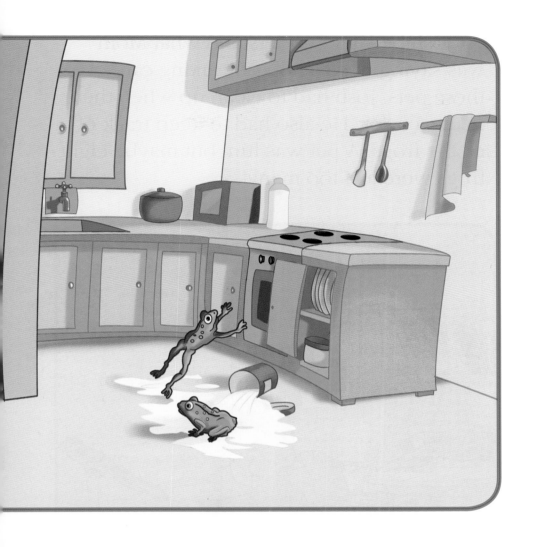

Josh thought about it. Hoppy 2 jumped on his homework and got it wet. Hoppy 3 spilled paint all over his desk. Hoppy 4 and Hoppy 5 liked to balance on the drawers. Hoppy 6 croaked all night. Hoppy 7 and Hoppy 8 jumped out of the bedroom and to the kitchen. They made a huge mess on the floor with flour and sugar.

Josh began to understand what Mom was saying. It was not easy taking care of all these pets. Josh had to clean up when they made a mess. He also had to keep track of all the frogs. A pet was fun, but maybe eight frogs were just too many!

The next day, Josh left Hoppy 1 at home, and Mom and he took the seven other frogs back to the pond. One Hoppy was enough for Josh. Now, he would have a pet to play with but no huge messes to clean up!

Frogs as Pets

Before you get a frog, decide how big of a frog you want. Some frogs grow to be very large.

Second, decide where your frog will live. Most people put their frogs in tanks. Some frogs need tanks that are half land and half water.

Next, find out what to feed your frog. Different frogs eat different things.

Finally, always make sure you wash your hands after touching your pet frog. There is so much to learn about having a frog as a pet.